Making Feedback Work

The Key to Building Effective Teams

Elaine Holland

ISBN: 978-1496103048

Printed in the United States of America

For Byrd Ball

My lifelong friend and mentor

For Stephen Parks

My twin brother who will always be in my heart

Contents

Introduction

Every manager is responsible for providing employees with feedback about their performance - both praise and suggestions for improvement. Yet too often, feedback misses the mark. It is either too vague or too late or it is not given at all.

Lack of feedback contributes to employees feeling disengaged. The facts are shocking: The Gallup 2013 State of the Global Workplace study concluded that "63% of the world's employees have essentially checked out, and an additional 24% are acting out their unhappiness and undermining the accomplishments of the 13% who are committed to innovation and organizational progress."

Feedback is important. It is a powerful yet underused management skill. It builds trust in relationships, contributes to professional growth and recognizes team members' skills and contributions. It also clears up misunderstandings, preventing small issues from growing into larger management challenges.

Too often managers avoid giving feedback because they are either unskilled, uncomfortable or don't want to hurt someone else's feelings. Yet avoiding potential confrontations just makes matters worse. And by failing to recognize your team's contributions, you run the risk of contributing to their disengagement.

This quick reference guide is a tool to help you build more effective teams with feedback. I know you're busy and your discretionary time is precious. Therefore, in the interest of brevity, each chapter has been organized so you can quickly find the information you need. You will find real-world examples, topical tutorials, a checklist for success and questions to help you make this material real and relevant.

CHAPTER 1

What
is
Feedback

Chapter 1 - What is Feedback?

"Feedback is the breakfast of champions."

~Ken Blanchard, author of *The One-Minute Manager*

As an IBM Sales Education manager, one of my instructors was a very talented, motivational speaker but not interested in teaching the more complex, technical topics. The team had been tolerating the situation for several years instead of giving him feedback on the impact of his behavior. After a few heartfelt discussions, he left IBM and went on to become a successful entrepreneur. He recently told me it was "the best decision he ever made". Our feedback discussion helped him unlock his personal success!

The best definition of feedback I've found comes from Charles N. Seashore, Edith W. Seashore and Gerald M. Weinberg in their book, *What Did You Say? The Art of Giving and Receiving Feedback*. They define feedback as:

- Information about past behavior;
- Delivered in the present;
- Which may influence future behavior.

Expanding on their definition, feedback also includes the following elements:

Feedback is given against a set of standards. For individuals and teams to be effective, there has to be a common commitment and purpose, performance goals and mutual accountability.

Standards include an agreement about the time frames, levels of effort, urgency and importance, and a plan for following up and monitoring progress.

Feedback is a two-way conversation during which we have the opportunity to see ourselves as others see us. It is a valuable source of information that helps us appreciate the impact our behaviors have on others and understand areas for learning and growth.

There are two types of feedback; positive and negative. Positive feedback is commonly perceived as a compliment. It is used to reinforce desired behaviors. Negative feedback is commonly perceived as a criticism and is used to draw attention to behaviors or performance that needs to change or improve. The meaning of the feedback, whether is it perceived as positive or negative, is determined by the person hearing the feedback.

Negative feedback has been called "constructive" or "developmental" feedback or "areas for improvement". In this guide, I will use these words interchangeably.

*This is an important point...***feedback should be given frequently** and not just during annual performance reviews. If the information provided during the performance review is a surprise, the manager has not been doing his or her job.

Feedback flows three ways: between a manager and employee, laterally between teammates and upward, from the employee to his or her manager. Therefore, this guide also includes tips for how to receive feedback.

Checklist for Effective Feedback:

- Your team has a clear understanding of the standards of performance.
- Your feedback discussions are a two-way conversation.
- You provide both positive and constructive feedback.
- You give feedback frequently.
- Feedback flows all three ways in your organization: between you and your direct reports, between the members of your team and from them to you.

Ask Yourself:

1. Recall a time you received effective feedback. What did the person do to make it easy to hear what they were saying?
2. Now recall a time when you were not receptive to the feedback. What would you have done if you were in the other person's place to make the experience more productive?
3. How frequently are you giving feedback?
4. Have you ever noticed that what you thought was a compliment was received as criticism or the other way around?
5. How could you make it easier for others to give you feedback?

CHAPTER 2

Why
Feedback
is
Important

Chapter 2 - Why Feedback is Important

"I remind myself every morning: Nothing I saw this day will teach me anything.
So if I'm going to learn, I must do it by listening."

Larry King – American television/radio host

I started playing the piano in the fifth grade. My piano teacher would reward me with a small bust of the composer after mastering a piece of music. After the summer break, I talked with a school friend and learned that she had earned 12 busts to my measly four. I've always wondered how much further I would have progressed that summer had I known that the standard for performance could have been four times my current rate of learning.

This story illustrates that without feedback, we don't know what is possible. In addition to the benefits already mentioned in the first chapter, there are several other reasons feedback is important, including:

Feedback promotes clarity and alignment among members of the team. Feedback is like the oil that keeps the car engine running smoothly. Your team will also grind to a halt without effective feedback.

Feedback is essential for learning and career development. Feedback provides guidance about which skills we need to develop or behaviors we should change. Without feedback, we don't know what to do to improve our performance.

Feedback is a source of motivation and promotes employee engagement. People like to know that what they're doing is important and feedback can also send the message that you're available to help.

Without feedback, people will fill the void with their own thoughts; either overly self-critical or congratulating themselves too much. Without feedback, people have to rely on external events to figure out how they are really perceived by the organization.

Feedback helps define your company or team culture. Chris McGoff provides a really clear definition of "culture" in his book, *The PRIMES: How Any Group Can Solve Any Problem.* His definition of culture is:

Behaviors We Tolerate

_____Culture_____

Behaviors We Do Not Tolerate

Feedback is a tool we use to discuss behaviors we do tolerate and don't tolerate. Without feedback, the culture of your team will be created by default.

"Culture" is just one of 32 PRIMES. In *The PRIMES book*, McGoff reveals universal patterns of human behavior. The PRIMES are, "32 bite-sized chunks of solid wisdom and proven expertise" from his work facilitating strategy session for over 10,000 government and industry professionals. *The PRIMES* is an excellent resource for any manager or leader.

Two Snapshot Examples: Why Feedback is Important

From the world of sports:

It is difficult to definitively measure the impact of feedback in the workplace. However, this example from the world of cycling demonstrates feedback's powerful impact.

In 1983, Bandura and Cervone carried out research on a group of cyclists. They split a group of 80 men and woman into four smaller training groups as such:

- The first group received clear performance goals.
- The second group did not receive goals but did receive regular performance feedback.
- The third group was given goals at the start and feedback throughout.
- The fourth group was the control and didn't receive goals or feedback.

The third group that received both goals and feedback improved nearly three times as much as the fourth group, which didn't receive either goals or feedback.

This illustrates shows just how important the giving of helpful feedback is to the development of individuals and the wider team.

my experience running a non-profit:

One employee asked another to help her move a box. When she declined, the employee with the box became upset. After all she had done, why couldn't she get the help she needed?

On the surface, it looked like a simple misunderstanding. However, over the next few days, the entire team had become polarized into two camps; those who supported the employee with the box and those who supported the one who said no.

This situation provided us with the opportunity to define how we intended to interact with each other. We asked, "What culture did we want to create?" We used several "PRIMES" from McGoff's book to guide the discussion and created agreements about how we intended to work together. The increase in team rapport, mutual respect and productivity was remarkable.

Ask Yourself:

1. What are the standards of performance you've set for the members of your team?
2. When have you checked in with your team about their progress toward their goals?
3. What positive and constructive feedback do you need to give to each member of your team?
4. What culture are you creating?

CHAPTER 3

How
to
Give
Feedback

Chapter 3 - How to Give Feedback

"Compassion is the basis of all morality."

~Arthur Schopenhauer – German philosopher

I lived in London for about four years, leading a 225-person sales and operations team located across Europe and the US. I started the senior leadership team's annual kick-off meeting by going around the room and publicly acknowledging each leader for his most significant accomplishment during the prior year. During the tea break, one person said, "That was the most embarrassing thing you could have done. Never do that again!" For many years, I attributed their reluctance for public recognition to a cultural difference. Recently, I learned that it has more to do with personal behavioral preferences than cultural norms. Adapting to other person's preferred communication style can increase the impact.

An Effective Feedback Model Has Three Steps

The three steps are:

Step One:	Identify the specific behavior
Step Two:	Describe the impact
Step Three:	Discuss the future desired behavior

Here are a few simple examples to demonstrate how both positive and constructive feedback includes all three parts:

Positive Feedback

"I noticed you submitted the report early, thank you!" (Specific Behavior)

"Now I'll be able to move forward with the project earlier than planned." (Impact)

"I appreciate your initiative and hope you'll continue to support the team in this way. " (Future Behavior)

Constructive Feedback

"I noticed you were ten minutes late to the last two meetings." (Specific Behavior)

"We had to start the meeting later than planned which inconvenienced the rest of the team." (Impact)

"Please be on time going forward." (Future Behavior)

Next, we'll go into a bit more detail of each step of the model.

Step One – Identify the Specific Behavior

The key to being specific is to observe what was actually said or done. Without knowing the specific action that led to the feedback, it is difficult to know what led to the praise or criticism.

One way to practice being specific is to think of the situation as if you were using a video camera to record what was said or actions that were performed. A video camera does not add any interpretation to the situation.

Appendix A lists some commonly used adjectives to describe people. There is nothing wrong with using adjectives; the key is to be able to substantiate them with specific observations to support the words you select. For example, if you describe someone as "ambitious", what are they doing or saying that leads you to that choice of descriptor?

It is very common to hear non-specific, subjective feedback. For example, "you did a great job" or "you are really talented" without saying what the person actually said or did to warrant the praise. Constructive feedback often falls in the same trap. Here are some common examples: "you just aren't a team player", or "you need to be more professional", or "more service-orientated", "more helpful", or "show more initiative".

Being specific is important. Without knowing what action or statement contributed to the assessment, the receiver of praise or criticism doesn't know what to continue to do or what to change.

Step Two – Describe the Impact

The second step of the feedback model describes the impact of the behavior. This is the easiest of the three steps of the model. The impact is generally what we feel first. For example, your reaction might be, "That was really terrific!" (Impact) You have to ask yourself - what made it terrific? (Specific Behavior)

This step of the model helps the employee understand the impact of his or her actions.

Step Three – Discuss the Future Desired Behavior

The third step of the model discusses the future desired behavior. It can either be an acknowledgement of positive behavior or a discussion of skills that can be built in the case of constructive feedback. A useful test is to ask: Do I know what I want them to do differently or continue doing as a result of this feedback?

The chart below shows a few more example of the Feedback Model. These examples may sound stiff or formulaic...they simply illustrate the model. You will want to adapt the process to your own conversational style.

Step One *Observation* of a Specific Behavior	Step Two The *Impact*	Step Three *Future Desired Behavior*
Your report was due Tuesday and it didn't arrive until Friday.	This delayed the budget consolidation process.	Timeliness is important. Let's talk about how to prioritize more effectively.
The charts you used to present the survey results were easy to read.	We were able to quickly see what actions need to be taken.	How we can use charts more frequently in other reports?
Your comments on the report weren't specific.	We aren't sure what needs to be done.	Please be clearer with your recommendations.

12 Additional Tips for Making Feedback Work

1. **Prepare - do your homework.** Feedback should not be a spontaneous event. Get the facts. Nothing destroys trust faster than unfairly criticizing someone. What actually happened? Were the expectations clear? Do you need to gather information from others?

2. **Have empathy for the person receiving the feedback.** No one likes to hear they've failed in some way. Changing behavior can be difficult, especially if you're asking them to take a look at an ingrained way of behaving. By making sure your intentions are to be helpful and you have empathy for the other person, you increase the odds of your message being heard.

3. **Be direct.** Don't sugarcoat negative feedback – if you aren't direct, your employee may leave confused about what you were trying to say, or misunderstand the seriousness of the situation.

4. **Make it a two-way conversation.** I realize that I've said this before but it bears repeating! After you've described the behavior and the impact, it's a good idea to pause so the person hearing the feedback has a chance to absorb what you're saying and possibly respond.

5. **Stay open.** Don't mistake valid reasons for excuses – listen to your employee's explanations about the situation and don't quickly dismiss what they're saying as an excuse or justification.

6. **Make sure positive feedback outweighs negative by a ratio of 5:1.** Your suggestions may be heard as criticisms. The trick is to catch them doing something right five times more often than pointing out what needs to be fixed.

7. **"I" versus "You".** When you start feedback with "you did this...", it immediately puts the receiver on the defensive. Instead, start with "I observed ...". This leaves the door open for additional information and sounds less confrontational and finite.

8. **Avoid absolutes.** Words like "always" or "never". The minute you generalize, your employee will find one example and use it as an excuse to discount the message.

9. **Start by describing the behavior (Step One) versus the impact (Step Two).** It is easier for someone to hear the behavior first. The receiver can quickly agree or disagree....i.e., 'yes, I was 10 minutes late'. It is hard to refute the facts. If you start with the impact (Step Two), it may put the receiver on the defensive.

10. **Follow-up.** Checking-in reinforces the positive behavior or continues to correct the problem behavior. Either way, you are sending the message that you were serious about your observations and that changing the behavior is important. Be sure you "Expect and Inspect."

11. **Make notes about your feedback.** Making notes helps you remember what you've said and identify

patterns of behavior over time. Notes will also help you when you prepare for an employee's annual performance review. Without notes, you run the risk of only assessing the most recent events.

12. **Avoid using the "Sandwich" approach.** Many sources suggest that you say "something positive, something negative and then something positive." The reason I don't suggest using the Sandwich approach is everyone knows what you're doing so your compliments come across as insincere and manipulative. Be direct about what isn't working and save positive feedback for another time. To learn more about why the Sandwich approach undermines your feedback, check out Roger Schwarz's April 19, 2013 HBR Blog: http://blogs.hbr.org/2013/04/the-sandwich-approach-undermin/

If you're upset...wait!

Here are three good reasons to get your emotions under control before giving someone feedback.

1. If you give feedback when you are upset, the receiver will feel judged and likely tune you out and become defensive.

   Prove this to yourself by recalling a time when you had an argument. Notice how easy it is to remember the emotion but not the content!

2. If your emotions are not under control, you may say something you will regret later.

3. The irony is, the more detached you are to changing someone's behavior, the more likely they are to make the change. This is why young people are more likely to listen to their peers than their parents. If you're upset, it is very difficult to remain detached.

Scheduling Time to Give Feedback

"Praise in public, criticize in private," is the Holy Grail of employee communications...or is it? Mark Horstman and Mike Auzenne are co-founders of Manager Tools LLC (http://www.manager-tools.com). They have created over 400 podcasts for managers. According to their experience, public praise is effective for only 50% of employees.

Behavioral specialist Laura Treonze says this can be explained through behavioral understanding and the DISC. People who process information internally are often embarrassed or uncomfortable with public praise and other forms of external recognition. If you want to know more about DISC, contact Laura Treonze at LMTworthtalkingabout.com.

I highly recommend Laura because of her in-depth knowledge of DISC. Her validation of your individual DISC results will increase your self-awareness and provide practical tools to improve communication at work.

Criticizing in private can create two problems; if you can't easily find a completely private place, you may have to delay the feedback. Today's open plan office environments make it difficult to find private space.

Instead of opting for complete privacy, Mike and Mark suggest that you can lower your voice and quickly give someone feedback while walking from one area to another.

Remember a time when your boss asked you to 'come see him or her in their office at a certain time'? And then you spent the hours between now and then thinking through everything you might have done wrong? No matter how minor the feedback, the actual act of walking to the office and closing the door ensuring complete privacy sends so many "this is VERY serious" signals. No matter how much you downplay the feedback, your employee will have imagined the worst and may be completely intimidated by the action.

For more on this, listen to Mark and Mike's Podcast: http://www.manager-tools.com/2010/06/praise-public-criticize-private-wrong

Bottom line – Give feedback as soon as possible and don't wait until you have a private place to do it. However, if you're upset, get your emotions under control first.

Future-based Feedback

Remember a time when someone was upset with you over something that happened in the past...and how awful you felt because there was nothing you could do about it? You can't turn back time or rewrite history. But you can focus on the future - the skills or behaviors you need to be more effective going forward.

Future-based feedback places more attention on future actions than the past. The two approaches below illustrate the difference between past-based versus future-based feedback.

Feedback that does not work puts too much emphasis on Step Two – talking about what didn't go well:

1. "You were late with the report."

2. "Therefore, I couldn't consolidate the budget and meet my deadline. This really reflects badly on all of us. It was a simple request and we go through the budgeting process every year. I don't understand why this was so hard to do."

   (Pause)

3. "Please don't let me down again."

Feedback that does work puts the emphasis on Step Three, the solution - new skills or behaviors that will occur in the future.

1. "You were late with the report."

2. "Therefore, I couldn't consolidate the budget and meet my deadline."

   (Pause)

3. "Let's talk about what we can do to make sure that you can meet your deadlines. What happened? (Listen) Time management is an important part of

your job. Let's talk about how you can develop this skill so going forward you are able to meet your deadlines by setting priorities, communicating more frequently or asking for help to resolve conflicting objectives."

Talking about future behaviors builds trust. You are sending the message that you're on their side; working with them and to help them improve. If the majority of your time is spent talking about the past, you may be inadvertently sending the message that their job may be in jeopardy.

Upward Feedback

Giving your boss feedback can be tricky. It takes courage to talk about sensitive issues, especially with someone you report to. However, you are doing you and your company a disservice if you tolerate any behavior that erodes the team's effectiveness.

It is very important for a manager to know how he or she is perceived. The higher someone is in the organization, the harder it is for them to get honest feedback. Your feedback can help your boss understand the impact of his/her behaviors and make the necessary adjustments.

During my career, I have benefited from upward feedback and strongly encourage you to talk to your boss about how he or she could improve.

Before you go into your boss' office with your list of suggestions, here are a few things to keep in mind (adapted from Amy Gallo's article, How to Give Your Boss Feedback):

Do:

- Be certain your boss is receptive before speaking up. Ask if he/she would like to hear your insight.
- Share specific information about your perceptions.
- Focus on his/her improvement and how you might help.

Do not:

- Assume you know or appreciate your boss' full situation.
- Talk about what you would do if you were the boss.
- Use feedback as payback for constructive feedback you may have received.

Snapshot Example: The Importance of Preparation

During my tenure as a Chief Talent Officer, I investigated a complaint; an employee alleged that a manager was "abusive and hostile".

The manager and employee's version of what had transpired was very different.

The manager said that over the previous six months, the employee was consistently late with her reports. He said he finally decided it was time to talk to his employee about the importance of getting her work done on time.

The employee reported that her manager spoke to her in an "abusive and hostile" tone, cut her off and would not listen to any explanations about why the report was late. She was so upset by the exchange, she requested a transfer to another team.

When I discussed the situation with the manager, he admitted that he had let several instances go and the most recent situation as "the last straw". Plus, he said that while his words may have been neutral, he admitted he had not kept his emotions in check and showed that he was upset.

I learned more from the employee as well. She told me she had been in an abusive marriage and was hypersensitive to anyone who was upset with her because she was too familiar with how the situation might get out of hand. She agreed she had over-reacted to the manager's tone.

This example illustrates:
- The importance of timely feedback; don't let it build up.
- Emotions always carry more impact and meaning than words.
- The person receiving the feedback will/may interpret what is said based on past experiences.

Remember: wait until you can put a smile on your face and approach the situation with curiosity. If feedback is given when you are upset, the person will feel the emotion and won't be able to hear the message.

Checklist for Giving Feedback:

- Prepare
- Wait if you're upset
- Ensure your intent is to help; be compassionate
- Be direct
- Use the model; Observation/Impact/Suggestion
- Spend more time on the future (Step Three) than the past (Step Two)
- Listen; make it a two-way conversation
- Make notes about the discussion
- Remember the 5:1 positive to negative ratio

Ask Yourself:

1. What are the future behaviors and skills you would like to see your team exhibit?
2. How can you apply the concept of "future-based" feedback to your next feedback conversation?
3. What feedback (if any) do you have for your boss?
4. How can you be more open to feedback from your team?

CHAPTER 4

Why Managers Avoid Giving Feedback

Chapter 4 - Why Managers Avoid Giving Feedback

"The future depends on what you do today."

~Mahatma Gandhi

I thought I had a perfectly good excuse for not giving an employee feedback – she didn't directly report to me, and we only had a dotted-line reporting relationship. So I asked her manager to give her the feedback. He did not present the feedback as his own. He transparently said, "Elaine said that you...". She was justified in feeling betrayed by me. It took several months before I discovered why we were having trouble working together. She had become reluctant to engage at the same level. Once we cleared the air about what happened, trust was restored and we were able to return to a productive working relationship. However, all of this could have been avoided if I had not avoided giving her the feedback.

Most managers avoid giving constructive feedback. Everyone wants to have good relationships with their work colleagues. Therefore, we hesitate to tell them what they could be doing better. How many times have you avoided giving feedback hoping the situation would resolve itself? Failing to give feedback will ultimately destroy trust and erode your team's effectiveness.

Here are ten of the most common excuses I've heard:

1. I don't want to hurt her feelings.

2. I don't think he can handle it.
3. Maybe this job just isn't a good fit. She might perform better if I move her to a new job.
4. What if he gets mad and quits?
5. I want her to like me.
6. I let it go before so I can't say anything now.
7. I don't want to derail my star performer.
8. It doesn't happen all the time.
9. Maybe she is just going through a bad phase.
10. I'm sure he already knows.

And the excuse I used in the example above and have heard from others...

It is not my job.

Unless teams are accountable to each other, team performance will suffer. The responsibility to give feedback is everyone's job. In today's highly-matrixed, global environment, everyone should recognize each other's accomplishments and discuss areas for improvement.

There are two key themes that contribute to why managers avoid feedback:

1. I don't know how to start. (competence)
2. I'm not sure I can handle the outcome. (confidence)

Competence is easy to develop. Follow the guidelines in this book, start practicing by giving positive feedback and work your way up to constructive feedback.

Building confidence is a bit more complex. It takes courage to give constructive feedback. Resources to build your confidence include your peers, a mentor, your HR professional or a coach.

And consider these points the next time you hesitate to give someone feedback:

- If you aren't telling the employees the truth, you're really holding back their career as well as your own. People seldom advance to senior levels of leadership without demonstrating the ability to build the competence of others.

- By assuming they can't handle the feedback, you are treating them like children, not adults. It is only fair that people are made aware of the impact of their actions.

- You are sending the signal that you don't care every time you let poor performance slide.

- If they aren't aware of the impact of their actions and you neglect to say something, it is actually cruel. The momentary hurt is a lot less painful than the longer-term loss they will experience when they fail to move forward in their careers or the project stalls, or worse yet, fails because you did not have the courage to address a problem behavior.

Failing to give feedback can undermine the trust and morale of your team. This is too high a cost to pay in order to avoid some short-lived discomfort.

Checklist for Giving Feedback:

- When you avoid giving feedback, it never turns out well.
- You can develop your feedback skills. (competence)
- Resources are available to help you build the confidence.
- Everyone on your team wants both positive and constructive feedback.
- Feedback indicates that you care.

Ask Yourself:

1. What is it costing you and your team if you fail to give them positive and constructive feedback?
2. What excuse do you use most often for not giving feedback?
3. Is it a matter of competence or confidence?
4. How are you going to build your competence?
5. What resources are available to help you build your confidence?

CHAPTER 5

When Feedback Does Not Work

Chapter 5 - When Feedback Does Not Work

"Success is the ability to go from failure to failure without losing your enthusiasm."

~Sir Winston Churchill

As a member of a large global team, the most efficient way to stay in touch is through frequent group conference calls. Our team leader decided to 'tell everyone at once' that the group was failing to meet a performance standard. Negative group feedback seldom works. Star performers think that they are doing something wrong. And those who need to improve deflect the message; not realizing the message was intended for them. The team was left confused and demoralized. And several talented people who felt unfairly judged ended up leaving the organization. Negative group feedback seldom has the intended impact and can actually make the situation worse.

In spite of our best efforts, feedback - both positive and negative - will sometimes fall on deaf ears. Stacey Finkelstein (Columbia University) and Ayelet Fishbach (University of Chicago) researched positive and negative feedback and concluded that novices prefer positive feedback because it increases their commitment and confidence, and experts prefer to know what they did wrong so they can correct their mistakes. So whether feedback works or not may be a function of their level of confidence and experience.

Here is some additional information about why positive and negative feedback sometimes does not work.

When positive feedback does not work

When we hear compliments or positive feedback, many of us will turn the compliment around, giving the credit to someone else or find a reason why the action doesn't warrant the compliment.

In the Seashore and Weinberg book, *What Did You Say? The Art of Giving and Receiving Feedback*, the authors attribute the behavior of deflecting positive feedback to rules we formed when we were four years old; specifically:

> "I must always be modest and never stand out."
> "I must never brag about myself."
> "If someone says something nice to you, they're trying to get something out of you."

Instead of denying, resisting, protesting, arguing or distorting the compliment, simply say "thank you!"

When negative feedback does not work

The main reason negative feedback doesn't always work is that our survival instincts take over. Next time you're criticized, mentally note your feeling and what you experience. This will give you a glimpse into what someone else might experience when receiving negative feedback.

Another inhibitor to change is that the pattern of behavior being critiqued may be a behavior that has served them well in the past. In effect, you're asking the person to give up his "winning formula."

The current trend is to avoid giving negative feedback because it is de-motivating and discouraging. I understand the advice to avoid giving negative feedback if the majority of the discussion is spent discussing what went wrong (Step Two) instead of the future behaviors (Step Three). When the focus is on the future and helping others improve, I don't see the risk.

You increase the odds of negative feedback working when it is linked to someone's motivations (why they work) and their goals (where they want to be) and framed in a way that they know what to do instead (clear action plan). Negative feedback framed in the right way at the right time can be very motivating.

Finally, in some cases, people just can't change. If that is the case, I have two suggestions:

1. Encourage them to develop skills that can serve as a substitute.

FYI: For Your Improvement is the best guide I've found for developing skills. Written by Michael Lombardo and Robert Eichinger in 1996, FYI is a research-based, experience test guide for leaders and managers. Mike Lombardo has over 30 years of experience in executive and management research and in executive coaching. Bob Eichinger is the Vice Chairman of the Korn/Ferry Institute for Korn/Ferry International. During his 40+ year career, he was working inside companies such as PepsiCo and Pillsbury, and as a consultant in Fortune 500 companies around the world.

Using *FYI* as a resource, you could choose to substitute one skill for another. For example, instead of directly improving your Listening skill, you may to choose to use one to three of 12 skills listed as potential substitutes for Listening. Those skills include Approachability, Caring about Direct Reports, Composure, Conflict Management, Delegation, Managing Diversity, Fairness to Direct Reports, Interpersonal Savvy, Motivating Others, Patience, Personal Disclosure or Building Effective Teams.

2. Learn more about how to create change in people. I highly recommend Tony Robbins' program, *Creating Lasting Change, the 7 Master Steps to Maximum Impact.* This is an excellent guide for building skills in influencing the thoughts, feelings, actions, behaviors and emotions of others. More information about this program can be found at: **http://www.tonyrobbins.com/products/career-advancement/creating-lasting-change/**

Feedback doesn't always work. The key is to learn from the failure and try again without losing your enthusiasm as Sir Winston Churchill wisely advised.

Ask Yourself:

1. When have you noticed someone deflecting positive feedback? What can you do to help them accept the praise?
2. When have you failed to help someone build the skills or behavior that would serve them better? Are there substitute skills that can be developed instead?
3. Have you been giving your more junior people sufficient positive feedback?

4. Have you been challenging your more senior people with developmental feedback?
5. If someone isn't responding to feedback, what pay-off might they may be getting for continuing to behave that way?

CHAPTER 6

Asking
for
Feedback

Chapter 6 – Asking for Feedback

"If I am through learning, I am through."

~John Wooden, American Hall of Fame basketball coach

I worked for Ross Perot selling technology outsourcing services in the Global Financial Services industry. When I joined the company, Perot Systems had just lost a significant opportunity and I was asked to review the deal, interview the customer and come back with a "lesson" worth the equivalent value of the lost deal.

Ross Perot believes that 'punishing honest mistakes stifles creativity.' My report uncovered a few important changes that needed to be made in the internal bid process. Mr. Perot taught me a valuable lesson; the only time you lose is when you fail to learn something.

Feedback is fundamental to self-development. Successful, effective leaders know how to solicit and accept feedback graciously. They understand that in order to learn, they need to know about the impact of their behavior. Learning how to solicit feedback is an essential skill.

Here are four techniques you can use to solicit feedback.

Technique 1 – Start, Stop, Keep

Ask three questions from three sources; your boss, your direct reports and your peers.

1. What should I start doing?

2. What should I stop doing?
3. What should I keep doing?

Technique 2 – Strengths, Blind Spots and Situations

Solicit the opinions of others by using questions about your strengths, blind spots and how you perform in various situations.

Strengths

- What are my greatest strengths?

- Which skills do you value most?

- What value do I provide?

Blind spots

- What behaviors are holding me back?

- When have I not met your expectations?

- If I were to change one thing, what would that be?

Situations

- In what situations do you see me making the greatest impact?

- When have you seen me struggle?

- What situations trigger stress or other negative reactions for me?

Technique 3 – Development Partner

You can create a Development Partner; a trusted friend, colleague or mentor – someone who will give you honest and direct feedback and will hold you accountable to the commitments you make. Ideally is it someone who can observe you and give you feedback shortly after the event.

One way to help someone give you feedback is by suggesting an area you know you may need to develop. For example, you can say, "I'm working on improving my listening skills. What have you noticed when you interact with me?" When you've already indicated you know you have weaknesses in a particular area, it makes it easier for someone to share their opinion with you.

Technique 4 – 360-Degree Feedback

360-degree feedback is a process through which you receive anonymous feedback from your boss, your peers, your direct reports and sometimes your customers. Talk to your Human Resources department about soliciting feedback for you and helping you interpret the results. This is particularly useful if you are feeling defensive or uncertain about the information you may receive. If you are defensive, you are unlikely to get the truth if you ask people directly for feedback. Your Human Resources professional can also help you construct a development plan for improvement.

Snapshot Example of Asking for Feedback:

When I was promoted into a general management position, I moved to London to assume responsibility for the Computing and Electronics sector which generated about $40m a year. I remember calling my mentor, Byrd Ball, and confessing that I didn't know what I was doing and was afraid they'd find out that I was a fraud. He laughed and said, "What makes you think that I knew what I was doing when I took over as the IBM branch manager in Hawaii?" What a relief! I thought I had to know how to do the job before I got the job. A mentor is an invaluable resource when you need feedback.

Ask Yourself:

1. What is the best feedback you've received from someone? What about going back and asking for more?

2. When someone has asked you for feedback, what did they do to make it easy for you?

3. Which of the four techniques for soliciting feedback appeals to you the most?

4. What is your plan for soliciting feedback?

5. Who do you know that could be your Development Partner?

Chapter 7

Receiving and Acting on Feedback

Chapter 7 – Receiving and Acting on Feedback

"Tell me and I forget. Teach me and I remember. Involve me and I learn."

~Benjamin Franklin – American scientist, author, inventor, statesman and diplomat

My first management role with IBM was leading a sales and support team in Albuquerque, New Mexico. We were responsible for the roll out of new products and after conducting an internal announcement meeting, one of my employees asked to speak to me. She was visibly upset when she told me that by disclosing all of the announcement highlights during the overview, I had "stolen her thunder". It was a humbling experience for a rookie manager to realize that my behavior had left a key member of my team feeling demoralized. I learned a valuable management lesson that day; as a manager, the focus is now on others, no longer on me. To learn more about this, I highly recommend Marshall Goldsmith's book, *What Got You Here Won't Get You There.*

It is normal to become defensive and sometimes hurt when you receive corrective feedback. It can be difficult to face aspects of yourself that can be improved. Your effectiveness will increase when you are able to acknowledge both your strengths and weaknesses. By being open to feedback, you have the opportunity to develop the skills and behaviors so you can contribute your best.

Learning to receive feedback effectively is just as important as giving feedback effectively. Feedback helps you improve; it is a source of learning. Plus, if you develop a talent for receiving feedback, people will more likely want to talk with you and say what might otherwise be left unspoken. Listening to and acting on feedback will lead to developing stronger relationships and being a more effective team member or manager.

Rick Mauer, in *The Feedback Toolkit*, talks about SARA, the four steps you may experience when you receive feedback. SARA is an acronym for **S**urprise, **A**nger, **R**ationalization and **A**cceptance.

Your first response may be shock or surprise and you aren't sure how to respond. This phase will pass so the best response at this point is no response. Next you may experience anger; again, don't take any action, rather know that this emotion will also pass. Anger is replaced by rationalization; at this point, you start to come up with excuses and explanations. And finally you'll get to acceptance when you're able to objectively determine which parts of the feedback to accept and which to reject.

One technique to move through the four phases more quickly is to control your focus through the use of powerful questions. The three powerful questions that I ask myself when caught up in uncomfortable emotions are:

- "What else could this mean?"
- "What is good about this?"
- "I'm glad this has happened because…".

These questions combined with a powerful belief that everything that happens to me in life is for my greater good have helped me navigate through the emotions of Surprise, Anger, Rationalization and get to Acceptance more quickly.

Here are a few tips for becoming a great receiver:

1. **Breathe:** If you focus on taking deep, even breaths, you reduce the normal stress response when hearing feedback. By focusing on your breathing, you return your focus to the present moment and away from any negative feelings you may have (i.e. fear, sadness, anger, insecurity).
2. **Be Open:** Being open means you are open to new ideas and different opinions. While it is understandable that you may want to put your guard up, the more you're able to stay open and receptive, the more likely you are to hear what is being said.
3. **Listen:** Listen to what is being said. Keep your focus on the message and avoid mentally rehearsing your response while they are still talking. Repeat what you've heard to ensure you've captured the key points. Ask questions for more information. Ask for specific examples. You will absorb more if you focus on understanding what is being said.
4. **Summarize your understanding:** Make sure you understand before responding. Paraphrasing what you've heard in your own words is a good way to ensure you have understood the message.
5. **Don't get defensive:** The minute you start to argue or act aggressively, you have lost. Nothing ever good comes from being rude, judgmental or combative with others, especially your boss.

6. **Apologize:** You may need to own your mistake and do what you can to rebuild the relationship and regain their trust.
7. **Reflect on what you've heard:** This is a key point; *you have the power to accept or reject the feedback.* Assess the consequences of acting on the feedback or ignoring it. Not all feedback is valid. Before you discount what was said, consider asking for a second opinion from someone else. You may need to take responsibility for your actions and the impact it had on others. We consciously don't intend for our actions to be misunderstood, but without feedback it is difficult to separate what we intended from the actual impact.
8. **Create a plan for moving forward:** Test your new approach with the person who gave you the feedback. Not only will you find out if you're on the right track, it also lets them know you've heard and appreciate their suggestions.

Now that you have received feedback, you can go to work on creating a plan to develop the new skills and behaviors.

I've already referenced *FYI: For Your Improvement* as an excellent guide for skill development. *FYI* should be on every manager's bookshelf. It is a 'must-have' book for anyone interested in career advancement.

Lombardo and Eichinger identified the 67 measureable characteristics that relate to success at work. A competency is:
- Behavioral skill
- Technical skill
- Attribute (i.e. intelligence)

- Attitude (i.e. optimism)

For example, let's say that you received feedback that you need to build more effective teams.

The chapter on Building Effective Teams includes:

- Competency definitions—unskilled, skilled and overused skill content
- Causes—numerous reasons why learners may have this need
- Leadership Architect® Factors and Clusters
- Remedies—ten or more tips to work directly on this need
- Develop-in-Place Assignments
- Suggested readings

Unfortunately, too many managers think the solution to developing skills is "send someone to a class". And the majority of the development plans in employee files are simply a list of classes the employee is scheduled to attend.

Lombardo and Eichinger's research shows that 70% of skill development comes from tough jobs, 20% from people (mostly the boss), and 10% from courses and reading. And my experience certainly proves this point; I've learned the most from doing the work.

Another valuable resource is your mentor or coach. Throughout my career, I've been able to talk to my mentor, Byrd, about any challenge. It has been incredibly helpful to have someone to talk to about everything from strategy to personnel issues.

Acting on feedback is an important step in developing the skills and expertise you need to advance in your career. By focusing on your goal (what you want to achieve) and by understanding why that goal is important to you, you'll find the motivation you need to create your personalized development plan.

Snapshot Example of Receiving and Acting on Feedback

A manager met with a talented, long-term employee to tell him his position had been eliminated. She was understandably concerned about having to deliver the bad news. While this isn't a typical feedback example, this illustrates how your reaction to bad news can have an impact on your future.

The manager explained that she had to drive some costs out of her group and reorganized the team, eliminating his position. The way he handled the discussion was remarkable. Instead of getting angry, he asked questions and expressed concern for the manager, recognizing how difficult this decision had to be. His empathy for her feelings was evident. And he managed to control his emotions and talk through his questions and options with her.

As a result, she redoubled her efforts to find another position for him in a different part of the company. After working on a temporary assignment until another role opened up, he was able to retain his position and has subsequently been promoted.

He was clearly a master of handling feedback. If he had reacted badly, blaming her for the decision, I doubt he would still be with the company today. Instead, by showing empathy, controlling his reaction and putting the interests of the company and his boss above his own, he was able to successfully navigate through a difficult time, ensuring his career continued to progress.

A Second Snapshot Example of Receiving and Acting on Feedback

A second Snapshot Example involves a colleague who presented a marketing strategy to a group of his colleagues. When they started to ask questions, he initially thought they were 'poking holes and taking pot shots' at his brilliant and well-constructed plan. He started to become defensive.

Then his boss asked him, "Wouldn't you rather learn about any holes in your strategy now instead of waiting until the market responds by not buying the product?"

By shifting his perspective from 'they're taking cheap shots' to 'this is an excellent early field testing opportunity', he was able to capitalize on the feedback. He became a good receiver with a simple shift in perspective.

Checklist for Receiving and Acting on Feedback:

- Listen
- Ask questions
- Manage your reactions
- Remember you have the power to accept or reject the feedback
- Apologize – if appropriate

- Focus on the future
- Create a plan for developing the skills you need
- Be grateful someone cared enough to give you feedback

Ask Yourself:

1. Remember a time you received feedback that was upsetting; how did you handle it?
2. If you were to do it over, what would you have done differently?
3. Which of the tips for handling feedback will be most useful for you in the future?
4. How do you plan to control your emotions the next time you receive disappointing news?
5. What perspective can you adopt in advance that will make it easier to hear feedback?
6. What is your plan for creating new skills and behaviors?

CHAPTER 8

Final
Thoughts

Chapter 8 - Final Thoughts

"Someone should tell us, right at the start of our lives, that we are dying. Then we might live life to the limit, every minute of every day. Do it! I say. Whatever you want to do, do it now!

~Michael Landon, Actor

Last year, I experienced a tremendous loss when my twin brother died from liver cancer. When I found out about his prognosis, I realized that if I had just three months to live, I wouldn't want to leave this world without having written this book about feedback.

During my career, I've witnessed too many situations that could easily have been resolved if people talked to each other about the impact of their positive or negative behaviors. I watched careers stagnate over interpersonal skill deficiencies that would have been easily addressed if they had just received effective feedback. I've seen both productive and unproductive teams. Productive teams are open and honest with each other about their mutual accountabilities and the impact of their actions.

It is my fervent hope that this short guide will provide you with the insights you need to start having meaningful conversations with your teams, your colleagues and your leaders.

Life is precious; this is not a dress rehearsal. I wish you all the best in your journey and please feel free to contact me if I can answer any questions. I'm open for your "feedback"!

Appendix A

The next time you use one of these words, test yourself to see if you can identify the specific behavior that led you to select this description.

Positive Descriptors	Negative Descriptors
ambitious	arrogant
bright	bitchy
communicative	bossy
considerate	careless
courageous	compulsive
creative	cynical
decisive	detached
determined	domineering
diplomatic	greedy
discreet	impatient
emotional	impolite
energetic	impulsive
forceful	inconsiderate
honest	indecisive
impartial	indiscreet
independent	inflexible
loyal	intolerant
optimistic	irresponsible
persistent	mean
powerful	patronizing
practical	pessimistic
pro-active	quick-tempered
reliable	rude
resourceful	selfish
self confident	stubborn
straightforward	thoughtless
tough	unkind
understanding	unreliable

Appendix B

Resources

Resources:

Introduction

Gallup State of the Global Workplace
http://www.gallup.com/strategicconsulting/164735/state-global-workplace.aspx

Chapter 1 – What is Feedback

Charles N. Seashore, Edith W. Seashore and Gerald M. Weinberg, *What Did You Say? The Art of Giving and Receiving Feedback* (Smashwords Edition, 2013)

Chapter 2 – Why Feedback is Important

Chris McGoff, *The Primes – How Any Group Can Solve Any Problem* (The Clearing, Inc., 2011)

Bandura and Cervone research
http://ypalchemy.com/topics/ULAu7UpjmhK9bPu6.html

Jon R. Katzenbach, Douglas K. Smith, *The Wisdom of Teams, Creating the High-Performance Organization* (McKinsey & Company Inc., 1993). *The Discipline of Teams*, Best of HBR 1993

Chapter 3 – How to Give Feedback

Roger Schwarz, *The Sandwich Approach*, (HBR Blog April 19, 2013) http://blogs.hbr.org/2013/04/the-sandwich-approach-undermin/

Mark Horstman and Mike Auzenne, Manager Tools (http://www.manager-tools.com)

Amy Gallo, *How to Give Your Boss Feedback* (HBR blog, May 24, 2010)

Chapter 5 – When Feedback Doesn't Work

Stacey R. Finkelstein and Ayelet Fishbach, *Tell Me What I Did Wrong: Experts Seek and Respond to Negative Feedback* (University of Chicago Press, 2011)

Michael M. Lombardo & Robert W. Eichinger, For Your Improvement (Lominger International: A Korn/Ferry Company, 1996 – 2009)

Tony Robbins, *Creating Lasting Change*
http://www.tonyrobbins.com/products/career-advancement/creating-lasting-change/

Chapter 7 – Receiving and Acting on Feedback

Marshall Goldsmith, *What Got You Here, Won't Get You There* (Hyperion, 2007)

Rick Mauer, *The Feedback Toolkit* (New York, Productivity Press, 2011)

Additional resources:

Jon R. Katzenbach, Douglas K. Smith, *The Wisdom of Teams: Creating the High-Performance Organization* (McKinsey & Company, Inc. 1993)

What Every Manager Should Know About Feedback Esther Derby (www.cio.com) April 19, 2007)

Byron Katie's Judge Your Neighbor worksheet (www.thework.com) to understand the role your perceptions play in your assessments of others.

Sloan R. Weitzel, *Feedback that Works, How to Build and Deliver Your Message* (Center for Creative Leadership, 2000)

About Elaine Holland

As an Executive and Personal Development Coach, Elaine works with both organizational leaders and individuals. During her 35-year corporate career, Elaine held senior leadership roles in the technology and marketing industries and has worked for IBM, BT, Perot Systems, WPP and Millward Brown. She has extensive experience in sales, general management and human resources. Elaine also served as Executive Director for Harmony Hill, a non-profit cancer retreat center after the 25-year founder stepped down. Elaine had served on the Board of Directors for eight years and assumed the leadership role during this important transition. (www.harmonyhill.org)

Elaine is a Results Coach for Robbins Research International. She also owns Executive Development Coaching and Consulting (www.coachelaine.com). She lives in Union, Washington with her three cats and is currently training for her 21st marathon.

Fourteen of Elaine's 20 marathons have raised money for cancer retreat scholarships at Harmony Hill. As a result, anyone with cancer and their caregiver can attend cancer retreats at no cost.

She plans to complete a marathon in each of the 50 States, continuing her support for Harmony Hill.

Made in the USA
San Bernardino, CA
15 March 2019